Redeemed
by the Light

Redeemed *by the* Light

WITH THE FAITH OF A MUSTARD SEED

By
Keith W. Rustin, Jr.

www.belleislebooks.com

Copyright 2014 by Keith W. Rustin Jr. No portion of this book may be reproduced or transmitted in any form whatsoever without prior written permission from the publisher, except in the case of brief quotations published in articles and reviews.

All rights reserved.

Printed in the United States of America.

ISBN: 978-1-9399301-2-5

Library of Congress Control Number: 2013949948

Published by
BELLE ISLE BOOKS
www.belleislebooks.com

I would like to dedicate this book to Jann Rustin. Jann has been my wife for over ten years. If not for her arrival in my life I would not be here with you.

Introduction

Once I arrived at this particular place it was clear how I got here. I could see through the dust of my past that my flesh had finally caught up to my spirit. I had been made whole. The good fight of faith could now begin, and I can tell you the story of faith personified. Even the seeds that are cast to the wind believe they can reach the ground. (Romans 10:17 says *"So then faith cometh by hearing, and hearing by the word of God"*) so hear from me, a recovering alcoholic, about what God can do. The lost can be found and the blind will see that faith personified can be you or me.

I could line up every biblical saying there is and it will mean nothing if you don't believe in Christ as the Son of God. You can't have faith if you don't believe and you won't see God if you don't have faith. Faith is defined in the Bible in the book of Hebrews and it says this: 11:1, *"Now faith is the substance of things hoped for, the evidence of things not seen."* Verse 11:3 goes on to say, *"Through faith we understand that the worlds were framed by the word of God, so that things, which are seen were not made of things which do appear."* Faith is the foundation for survival in the world as a Christian. Through faith, life as God intended for his people is possible no matter what comes your way.

Both the beginning and the end lie in the same place. Life is cyclical and you can easily find yourself starting over with the wrong decision in life. We need not search high and low for something that we already possess as a gift from the Creator. What I'm saying to all who will listen is that the Kingdom of Heaven is within us all. But we all seek it, search for it, run from it, or try to pay for it when we have it all the time. If you can believe He is in me, you will know He is there with you, too. He will do for you what He has done for me. Christ forgave the sins of the world long before you will have read this story.

I have been redeemed from the hand of the enemy, which means I know of what I speak. I don't know any other way to say that Satan had me. Life was tumbling down a rabbit hole and it seems as if there was nothing I could do about it. Fortunately, God would not let Satan have me and He made a way out of the enemy's hand. Just as life is a process, so redemption is a process and that is where the healing lies.

There have been many people who have prayed for me over the years because I have been wandering the desert places of my life lost and without hope for some time, like the Israelites who were set free with no place to go. They were set free because of their faith, even though their eyes could not see the power they possessed. The believers in Christ can be free indeed, if we would stop and listen to what God has to say to us. We allow this world to toss us to and fro, like a staggering drunk.

A cliché does not become trite without being used for a purpose for a long time. The expression, "There's nothing new under the sun" is as true today as whenever it was first said. Psalm 107 was my story before it even happened. It says in verse 14 of Psalm 107, *"He brought them out of darkness and be thankful for His steadfast love."* He did just that for me with steadfast love. We have to understand that with God all things are possible (Matthew 19:26). This time my prayer is that you can see what I see: Everything God does is for Himself and He is in control of it all.

What does it take to believe? Would all have faith if they could see it, touch it or feel it? What if faith was made real? Come. Let me tell you the tale of faith personified and then you can decide.

Everything Means Something

Why are there always more questions than answers? When I turned fifteen, a metamorphosis of circumstance changed my life forever. My questions were as follows: Was life changing or was I? Had I made the right decisions? Did something happen to send my life astray? I ask these somewhat theoretical questions because the seemingly random chaos of life is not random at all. It's only when you take past events and string them together like popcorn that you see that they happened that way for a purpose—your purpose. From the beginning, every time I've changed my mind, I've changed my relationship to time.

Now if you believe that your relation to time is governed by the decisions you make and the direction you go, and combine it with the belief in Christ as the beginning and the end, then life begins to come alive. You see that everything happens for a reason, beginning with an idea that time manifests itself into reality and becomes more than you ever imagined.

My friend Alvin lived across the street from me on Cleary Road. We were teenagers then, and with summer coming to a close we were up late pretending to watch TV. The Jerry Lewis Muscular Dystrophy telethon was on television. That was the one program where you could see all kinds of entertainers.

We were looking up at the stars and contemplating our future. We were wondering just what God could do, and what it must be like to have that kind of power. Most of all, we were confirming the power He has over us. Well, *I* was anyway. I was telling Alvin about a rock band called Parliament-Funkadelic. My cousin had told me about them, and they were blowing my mind. There was a sound about them that I just couldn't get enough of.

One song in particular, "Good Thoughts, Bad Thoughts," seeped into my spirit. It stayed with me and spoke to me of what life could be or will be—I was never really sure which. ("Good Thoughts, Bad Thoughts." *Standing on The Verge of Getting It On.* Clinton, George. Cook, Grace. Westbound Records, 1974.)

Travel like a king.

Listen to the inner voice, a higher wisdom is at work for you. Conquering the stumbling blocks comes easier when the conqueror is in tune with the infinite.

Every ending is a new beginning. Life is an endless unfolding. Change your mind and you change your relation to time. You can find the answer. The Solution lies within the problem. The answer is in every question.

An attitude is all you need to rise and walk away. Inspire yourself. Your life is yours. It fits you like your skin.

The Oak sleeps in the acorn; that giant Sequoia tree sleeps in its tiny seed. The bird waits in the egg; God waits for his unfolding in man. Fly on, children.

You gravitate to that which you secretly love most. You meet in life the exact reproduction of your own thoughts. There is no chance, coincidence or accident in a world ruled by law and divine Order.

You rise as high as your dominant aspiration. You descend to the level of your lowest concept of yourself. Free your mind and your ass will follow.

The infinite intelligence within you knows the answer. Its nature is to respond to your thoughts. Be careful of the thought seeds you plant in the garden of your mind for seeds grow after their kind.

Every thought felt as true or allowed to be accepted as true by your conscious mind takes root in your subconscious, blossoming sooner or later into an act and bears its own fruit.

Good thoughts bring forth good fruit; bullshit thoughts rot your flesh. Think right and you can fly, the kingdom of heaven is within, free your mind and your ass will follow.

Play on children.

Alvin said, "Are you kidding me. What does that even mean?"

I responded, "I'm not sure, but I'm sure it means something. I'll let you know when I figure it out."

I hope to see Alvin someday to share with him what I've learned about that song. Until then I can share it with you, and hopefully you will come to believe what faith can do. Let's start at the beginning.

Life in the 1950s was challenging. I was born in Richmond, Virginia, the capital of the Confederacy. There was great hardship for some, but we survived. I've always seen my family as average middle class, though one could argue there was nothing average about a black family during the Civil Rights Era. I've always been very proud of my family. In fact, I've said many times, "I'm proud to be a Rustin." The things that were important to my family affected my childhood development. The things that were important to my grandparents are what are important to me now.

Growing up in the suburbs of Richmond, I knew of

no man more respected than my grandfather. In my fifty-two years I've yet to meet someone who commanded as much respect upon entering a room as he did. "Big Daddy" was what I called my grandfather, and for good reason, because he was the man. At least, as far as I was concerned, he was the man I wanted be. I wanted to be well respected in everything I did because it was clear to me as a youngster, or "The Boy," as he referred to me, that he was respected just because of who he was. What I didn't know is what he had to go through to be who he was as a person. Everything he said to me would be played over in my mind as if he had placed the key to wisdom and truth in my spirit to be called on at a later date.

One Saturday, my uncle, grandfather and I were on our way home from a fishing trip in Hampton Roads, Virginia. We were towing the boat that my grandfather owned back to Sandston, Virginia, and we made our regular stop at Washington's store. Washington's store was your normal country store on Route 238. My grandfather seemed to know everyone whenever we stopped there. One day this guy was over in the corner playing checkers with Mr. Washington and had a question for Big Daddy.

"What's going on up at the church?" he asked.

The answer was noteworthy, but not as much as the reaction to the question by everyone in the store. Everyone in the room—all six or eight people—stopped what they were doing as if in a trance and fixed on what Big Daddy had to say. You could hear a pin drop in the store. His answer was deliberate, but somewhat calculating.

"Don't judge what's going on at the church by what I say. Go to the church and see for yourself. Because what's up at the church for me is not the same for you. I wouldn't want you to miss out on your own blessing." I guess what Big Daddy said meant something to the people in the room because there was some murmuring and shuffling around after he spoke. That was the day I knew I wanted to be like Big Daddy, and someday people would hang on every word I said as well.

In fact, I've always strived to become like my grandfather. What I discovered was, I was looking in the wrong place.

Time has allowed me to find my way. However, I often feel time is running out and I have wasted so much of it. Where is the meaning of my suffering, the torment of grieving the loss of a life unfulfilled? The good news is that I've found a power beyond anything I've ever known. That power is in Christ, Jesus Christ.

Connected to the Vine

Some lessons can only be taught by Christ, but I believe all lessons learned are for His purpose. That is, when—and if—they are learned.

I've found that lessons will repeat themselves until they are learned. They'll just keep knocking you upside the head until, finally, a light bulb goes off, and you get it. This sounds a little cynical, but it's true nonetheless. The first lesson I encountered was that everything isn't always what it seems. It would take me years to figure this out. Turns out there were things I had to learn before growing into the next phase of my life. I'll give you an example of what I mean.

Can a child move on to the 11th grade in high school without the knowledge gained in the 10th grade? Maybe. But, even if this child gets into the 11th grade, we can agree that the 11th grade would be a struggle. And it certainly would be difficult for this child to reach the 12th grade. This is what happened to me.

I've struggled throughout life because I wasn't a willing participant in my own destiny. I never wanted to be present or experience what life was sending my way. But experiences in life are collected. They fit together like building blocks to create the structure on which our lives are built. These building blocks of life are one lesson built upon another.

This foundation of learning and growth shapes us into who we will become. When we choose to believe that God is at the head of our journey, we can achieve anything that can be imagined. I know that now. Would I know any more if I knew it then?

Life for me was fishing in the summer and hunting in the fall. That's what my family did, and I loved it. In 1971, the year I turned fourteen, I was going deer hunting for the first time, and I killed a three-and-a-half-year-old, eight-point buck. I was hooked for life on deer hunting. Hunting and fishing were more than family hobbies though; they were a way of life for several generations in the part of Virginia where I grew up. There were sports in my life, but nothing had appeal like the outdoors. I was not very good at sports, which may have something to do with the way I felt about it. Hunting and fishing were things I did well.

The way I view life today is not much different. The things I can't do very well I try to avoid (for example, dancing). This may not be the best of lessons. However, the lessons I've learned in life, good or bad, shape the person I am.

* * *

My grandparents had roots in the Mattaponi and Pamunkey Indian tribes of King William County, Virginia. They learned to hunt and fish the same way the Indians had for years. The Indians lived through a combination of fishing, trapping, hunting and farming. Hunting was a way to put food on the table in the fall and winter. It also gave people the chance to participate in a sport where they controlled their own destiny. All I needed was a shotgun, a hunting license and a legal place to hunt.

My grandfather worked for a man named Heckler, who owned a big farm in New Kent County, Virginia. We had permission to hunt and fish there any time we wanted. This farm was a sportsman's paradise and the very thought of a trip to the farm would spark excitement and anticipation in me. I could always count on seeing wildlife on the farm, whether it was white-tailed deer, fox, turkey or rabbit. At a time when minorities had few rights in America, they could own a gun and hunt for their own food. Perhaps this is why the generations that continue this tradition see it as a right as much as a privilege.

In the spring we would go to the farm and drift net fish

from a rowboat. Drift netting is a fishing technique where gill nets are floated down the river with the tide. While my grandfather and uncle would fish with the boat, my cousins and I would fish for catfish from the bridge at the creek. We were like Huckleberry Finn, only not as carefree.

Around one part of the farm, the Pamunkey River takes a big turn, like a crescent moon. My uncle would guide the boat as my grandfather fed the net into the water. Starting up the river, they would lay the net across the river, and let the it drift downstream with the outgoing tide. The trick was picking the net up before it went too far around the bend.

We would go to the farm every Saturday between late March and early June. The fishing trip started as soon as school was out on Friday. From that point everything was about Saturday morning. Most of the time my father would take me to my grandparents' house Friday evening. Once in a while my grandfather would come by and pick me up, and then we would stop and get my cousin George. He was the oldest of my cousins. Riding with my grandfather was always a treat because he had a pickup truck, and George and I would ride in the back. This was before riding a kid around in a truck bed was illegal. It was fun, though.

Our first priority was digging worms for bait. If it

was nighttime when we got to my grandfather's house, I would have to get up a little earlier on Saturday to dig the worms. The trip to the farm was always special, but one has stood out over time. It wasn't the trip as much as what waited for me when it was over. That particular day was as good as it got.

* * *

It was the summer of 1972 when everything changed. I came home from fishing with my grandfather, and discovered my mother was gone. Now, I don't mean she went to the store. I mean she had packed her clothes and shoes and moved out. I certainly didn't see it coming and I don't recall feeling much about it. I wonder if that day is so etched in my mind because Christ wanted to cushion the events that happened when my mother left. Christ knew she would leave and made a day of fishing a good one. God was watching over me long before I believed in Him. Faith is about choosing to believe.

However, the events that followed mom's leaving did leave a mark. Dad took mom's abandonment of us pretty hard. His struggle meant I had to step into a role that was not intended for a fifteen-year old. But, step up I did. Once that happened, presto, I lost the remainder of my childhood. Whether for better or worse, the veil of childhood had been lifted.

There was no way to know my father would fall apart after my mom left. He started drinking. He was seeking a message in a bottle. I was left to care for myself, and I did. I cooked, cleaned, washed my clothes and his, and when he was sober, I would get him to sign a few checks so that I could pay the bills and buy food. I was the towel boy on the varsity basketball team at the same time; I was in the 10th grade. I remember dad trying to get the people at the store to let me buy him beer once I got my license. I guess since I was buying our food there he thought it would fly.

His drinking was not pretty. Saturday or Sunday mornings were often *go find where dad left the car* or w*here's dad? Oh, Jimmy's bringing him home. I wonder if he will take me back to his house to get the car.* Sometimes I would get teased that I was having Schlitz soup for dinner. (That was a beer from back in the '60s and '70s.) I might have, but I was doing the cooking.

If my father knows what precipitated my mother's exodus, he's not talking. In forty-seven years I haven't asked. Since that time I've felt the loss of a childhood I'm not sure I ever had. When a child is lost, even for a short time, we all suffer. I was set adrift and truly tossed to and fro. My father recovered after a year and a half. He got remarried and put his life back on track. I, however, did not recover quite so quickly. My focus on school suffered and I skipped a lot of school days. The last two school years

I missed over eighty days of school. I don't know what I thought was going to happen, but I didn't graduate from high school and it was a shock when I got the call.

Inside the Merry-Go-Round

Life began to teach me things about the world that I didn't want to know. I see now the experiences taught me who was in control. It turns out it wasn't me. It seems only Christ can make the right decision every time. This lesson took a while to learn. I joined the U.S. Navy to try and find some structure, or, it just seemed like a good idea at the time. I never took the time to see the opportunity as positive. My girlfriend was pregnant before I knew it, and so we got married. And I was kicked out of the Navy within fifteen months, because I missed an assignment to deploy to Puerto Rico.

Then,

My wife, my baby and I lived with my mother and her new husband for a while.

Then,

My mom kicked my wife out. I had been thinking about going to school when it happened, but I went to work instead.

Then,

I stayed with my wife for eight years although she hated me for seven of them. We cheated on each other. Eventually I left her for someone whom I really loved and who loved me.

Then,

I went to Delaware to work—with my new girlfriend, Evella, in tow.

Then,

I started cooking the cocaine and smoking the crack. I lost my apartment and my mom had to come get us out of Delaware.

Then,

I went back to D.C. I continued working and smoking crack.

Then,

I was robbed while buying crack. Twice.

Then,

My girlfriend cheated on me and broke my heart. Then she put me out.

Then,

I went back to Richmond with my father on Father's Day.

Then,

I tried to get back in the Navy, but I smoked crack the night before and never made it.

I got a job, met a woman in a bar, and smoked more crack. My father put me out and I lost my job.

Then,

I slept in my car for a while.

Then,

I met a woman named Kitty at a bar, who turned out to be what I call now a high-class junkie—and I was along for the ride. I loaned my car out to some dealers for a weekend for an eight ball of cocaine. That night I slept next to a dresser that cracked from the roaches inside of it. My clothes were in garbage bags in the trunk of my car until the dealers who had my car stole my stuff and sold it. I did get the car back, though.

Then,

I started driving for a guy named Robert who boosted

during the day. (Boosting is the street name for shoplifting.) Anyway, we would drive to 7-Eleven stores in rural areas and Robert would go inside and steal cigarettes. He would bring one or two cartons to the car per trip and sometimes make two or three trips. I would then drive us to another store where he thought he could get away with stuffing something down his pants that we could sell later. Sometimes we would find an auto parts store; it seems tools were a good seller. We smoked crack at night.

Then,

They stole my radio and my only suit. Without a suit I had no chance to get a real job, so I went back to Richmond and found Kitty.

Then,

I was looking for a life raft; so back to my mother I went. Now, it was the junkie and me—a want-to-be junkie—sleeping on my mother's floor. Mom paid the first week's rent for a room that Kitty had found in D.C. The room happened to be in the northeast D.C. neighborhood of Rayful Edmond, the biggest drug kingpin D.C. had ever seen. My junkie girlfriend put me right under the bus, got behind the wheel and ran me down. One night we were out and she was trying to run a con on somebody and I was looking for a way out. We were at a bar named Blackies. While she was trying to find someone to con into buying some crack, I was trying to find someone to take me home. It's all a little hazy. That night I found a way out of my situation. Safety was my primary goal back then. Her name was Katrina. I went to her apartment one time and got an offer to move in with her and her two kids. The choice was not hard at all. High-class junkie or lady-with-kids-in-tow were my only two options, so I never saw Kitty again.

Then,

Katrina became pregnant before you could say "are you my new daddy," and we named her Tabatha Pearl. Everybody calls her Pearl, unless she's in trouble. I knew I didn't love Katrina but she had just saved my life and I wanted my child to have my last name. So, I married her. This is when my drinking became worse. I was ashamed. I started to try to hide it. I was drunk so often that sometimes I was drunk without even knowing it. I thought I was normal. I hid half-pint vodka bottles anywhere I thought they were safe.

Our relationship ended when she put me in the hospital. What a night. I ended up with six stitches. You know it's bad when you hear the doctor tell the nurse, "Let's get him cleaned up so his mother doesn't see him like this."

Then,

Back to my mom. I got back with my first wife for about a week or so during this period. But off to mom's it was. I was battered and bruised, so mom took me in and patched me up. The woman I left my first wife for, Evella, had called mom and left her number. Her mother had died and so now she had her own place. I did still love her, but she had another child. The break-up between her and her baby's daddy was not pretty at all, but we were together once again.

Then,

I tried to get some help with my drinking by interviewing for a program. I explained to the counselor some of the things that were happening at the time, but mostly I complained about the merry-go-round in my head. I could not have been lonelier. This may sound vague and a bit psychotic, but everything in my life up to that point was spinning through my head constantly. It was a constant haze. It was like standing in the eye of a tornado. Think of the tornado as a cloud spinning in your head. I could see over and under the cloud, but everything in my life was swirling in the cloud, and I could see into every event of my past. They told me it was alcohol-related.

This time there was a house, kids and responsibility. This was round two with Evella. It was more like riding a wave. I didn't know where I would be when it was over. I just wanted to survive and be safe.

During this time I lost three jobs because of my irresponsible behavior. Luckily, I stayed with the last one long enough to receive insurance. The people I worked for made me get help. This gave me my first real shot to stop drinking. The crack was addicting in a different way somehow. I could take or leave it because it was a hassle and dangerous. The alcohol was a different story. This stuff was like magic. It would make all your cares go away and it was legal. It was also socially accepted, so what could go wrong?

I was going to therapy regularly. I met with a Mr. Goodall once for an assessment. He was recommended by my insurance company. I would then attend weekly group therapy sessions. One long night of drinking brought everything to a halt. When I didn't make it to work the next day, they fired me. Then I checked into rehab.

I was in rehab for a week. When the program ended I was taken back to Mr. Goodall's office, where we had our second consultation. I remember having my first laugh in some time when the counselor told me he would show me how to be happy without drinking. I wasn't very optimistic. Because I had been struggling for so long I didn't see being happy as a real possibility. Being drunk was easier. The fact that I was fresh out of detox, however, allowed me to really pay attention to what was being told to me in my sessions. I wasn't quite sure what had happened, but I knew what had to be done. I took what I was told and tried to make the changes that were necessary to stay sober. Through my sessions, it was determined that I suffered from depression and codependency. I had to let Evella go and make it on my own. It was easier said than done, but I had to try.

I was going to AA meetings at a few places around Falls Church, Virginia. One day I went to a meeting in the basement of a church in Vienna, Virginia and I was sharing with the group about this thing spinning around in my head. There was an old man, Mr. Abraham, who sat in the back but never shared very much. He stopped me at the end of the meeting and told me there was a man he had heard of that might be able to help.

I asked this old guy why he thought this man could help me.

He said, "He was my therapist when I was a kid. He used to say he could help anyone who wanted to be helped. Well, do you?"

"Of course, what's his name?" I asked.

"His name is Mr. Yahweh," he told me.

I knew the old guy sitting in the back of the room used to be a rabbi. If he can fall, no one is safe from alcohol. Mr. Abraham told me that Mr. Yahweh lived right in Vienna and he gave me the number.

I told myself this could be the person to help with this merry-go-round thing that was going on in my head. But if nobody knew what it was, how could anybody help?

Mr. Abraham told me that Mr. Yahweh used to be a teacher in Jerusalem. He came to the United States because his children were in trouble here in the states.

I called Mr. Yahweh soon after and made an appointment to meet at his home. He was a heavy set, slightly balding man with the most amazing blue eyes you have ever seen. He made me feel at ease the moment I saw him, as if I already knew he was there to help me.

"Come and sit down," he said.

I briefly explained to him why I wanted to see him. I told him of the spinning cloud in my head and tried to tell him what it looked like. When I finished telling him how my life was whirling around in my head like a TV left on in a tornado, he paused, made a few notes, and without much thought said, "It is not a cloud or a whirlwind but a pillar of cloud and fire. It's called the forge of Baal-Zephon. Baal-Zephon is the place by the Red Sea where the Israelites camped before Moses parted the sea for them to pass through on dry land. When the Israelites were saved from the Egyptians, it was the first time that they understood the power of their God. The pillar of cloud and fire that led the Israelites through the wilderness is this same pillar that guides his children who are lost even today."

"Why is it called the forge of Baal-Zephon?" I asked.

"Because the pillar of cloud that led the Israelites by day showed them the way, and by night the pillar of fire gave them light so they could travel around the clock. But, for us the pillar does something different. Now while the pillar still shows us the way, it works from within along with the Holy Spirit to purge us of the lessons in our life and forge them into wisdom from Him. It is said that when wisdom is forged by God that it is only for His use."

Mr. Yahweh continued.

"Baal-Zephon was the place where the Spirit of God first moved the pillar behind the children of Israel and they moved in front of the Spirit. This was their first choice in His presence. Because they were before Jesus Christ, the Holy Spirit had not come to them and the choices were outward. Now we have the Holy Spirit and God can work with us inwardly as individuals. We learn individual lessons and make choices in the same manner."

I asked Mr. Yahweh, "Is God telling me something with this pillar?"

"No," he said. "I would say it's more like it's taking you someplace."

"Can you tell me where?" I asked.

"No, I'm no prophet. What I can tell you is, He probably has a specific place for you to be and a specific thing for you to learn before you get there. What I do know is, because it's your past that's being forged, it's probably for someone's future. Nothing goes to waste with God."

Lessons Repeat Themselves Until Learned…

When I stopped drinking the first time, it set off a chain of events that only became clear in hindsight. These events would lead me to find the inspiration to rise and walk away from a life of hopelessness. I was trying to preserve my sobriety.

I have never lacked confidence. However, even though I had been beaten and battered around for a while, I refused to give up. I don't know how it happened, but I found myself in a place where I could take another shot at life. I wanted to figure out a way that I could at the very least live a safe life, a life that's going forward. I wanted to live a life that could make a difference in the lives of others.

The very thought that my life could really matter was exciting for me. It was the reason I was the manager of the varsity basketball team in high school. I'm nobody special. I didn't care about grades when I was in school. I wasn't very good at sports. I wasn't a standout with the girls. But if I could become the manager of the basketball team my picture would be framed and displayed in the lobby of the school gym inside a glass trophy case for as long as they keep old pictures. In some small way, I would have made a mark. That thought process has stayed with me my whole life. I will always feel like I have the potential to make a difference somewhere for someone, so I have to try.

Eventually I went back to live with my mother. I wasn't drinking and I was going to AA meetings every now and then. I had mixed emotions about the way AA was structured because they believe that nothing will help you unless you want help.

Regardless of what I was doing, whether it was drinking cheap vodka or smoking crack in a stairwell, I certainly did not want to be a drunk. There had to be more to a drunk like me or people like me than to just want it. There is a process to sobriety. Everyone can't use the same path, but everyone hopes to get to the same place.

I found a job working as a cook at a Cajun restaurant in Alexandria, Virginia. I wasn't the chef or the boss. There were no expectations or pressures. I felt my sobriety would be safe for a while, and it was a beginning.

I may have been a drunk in the past, but I was also an experienced chef. The job was perfect in several ways: it was challenging, it was a new cuisine, and there were people there who wanted to teach me. The business owners believed in teaching the staff how to run the operation correctly. There was an experienced chef on site. I fit right in. I did my job and I worked hard.

It wasn't long before employee turnover began. This happens a lot in the food service business. First one or two cooks left the company. Then a few weeks later the chef who was training me decided to quit. He wanted to go back to Alabama. He recommended me for his job. I could have turned the job down, but I stepped up and took it. I found out during this short period of sobriety that I was one hell of a cook. When my mind was clear, I proved to be a good leader as well. I was pleased for the recognition, and I ran the kitchen, ordered the food, hired people, and trained and promoted the staff. These were things that I enjoyed doing. The next year the restaurant I worked at was the only Cajun restaurant in the Washington area to be written up in the top 100 restaurants edition of the *Washingtonian Magazine*.

It wasn't too long after the review came out that one of my paychecks bounced. This is a very bad sign for any business. Payday became a stressful day. The day shift would be back at the restaurant before the dinner shift could start. They would come back and tell me there was no money in the account. The pressure began. I knew from experience what was about to happen. The restaurant group we worked for had three operations. And, sure enough, they lost one of them. I immediately started looking for another job and told the staff to do the same.

I ultimately left the job in Alexandria, Virginia for a restaurant in Washington, D.C. that served the same type of food. The food at the new restaurant was not as authentic as the one in Alexandria, but the businesses must have been run about the same.

The owner of the restaurant in Washington D.C. did some catering as well as running the restaurant. We were at a catering event when I met a lady named Mary who lived in Gaithersburg, Maryland. While I was getting to know Mary, the restaurant in D.C. began to have financial problems. The paychecks began to bounce just like before. Subsequently, I had to find a new job

One thing I figured out while I was in rehab was that I had to do things for myself. I was around thirty-five years old and I had never lived alone. I've lived with one woman after the next my whole life, so I decided to rent a room in D.C. and live on my own for the first time. I celebrated by buying my first television set. This seemed like the right direction.

It is hard to stay focused on something when you don't know how. Eventually I let Mary from Gaithersburg, Maryland talk me in to moving in with her. The townhouse she lived in was far better than the condition of the room I was renting. This seemed like an upgrade in my circumstance and the right move. Time seemed to be in my favor. I had a comfortable place to live. I had a new job as a chef where I could grow and learn. Life had a new rhythm.

The rhythm of life can only be sustained if the right music is playing. I know that now, but I didn't know it then. One day, Mary from told me, "We need to talk," and I listened. She told me she didn't want to be in a relationship with me anymore. There was no reason and no debate. I simply said, "Well, does that mean I have to move?" She said, "No, you can stay until you find someplace to go.

When I was in rehab for my drinking, I was asked what my trigger would be—what would cause me to start drinking again. I said the death of my parents, but I was wrong. Instead it was an emotional attack on my spirit. I was not prepared. I retreated to a place I thought I would be safe again: the light plastic $2.00 bottle of vodka that I knew I could count on to tuck me in every night.

Evella had been with me when I went to rehab previously. She was having some domestic issues and called me for help. I used her situation to propel me out of the one I was in. The opportunity to go backwards in life will always be there, because complacency is the enemy of change, and life can't go forward without change. I moved in with Evella. This time we slept in different beds.

My drinking was worse now. I knew I had a problem. I tried to hide how much I drank in a day by hiding the bottles in the house until I could safely throw them out without being discovered. If I just threw them in the trash, someone would know how much I drank. I would go to the liquor store every day, but I never went to the same one two times in a row. It was shame. I was ashamed of myself. I guess I really was living in a bottle. Gil Scott Heron wrote a song that said those very words. It looks like I was not the first to choose this type of life.

One day while I was driving on the Capitol Beltway I was struck by what could only be described as déjà vu. It seemed to me that I had been in this situation before and that I was sure how it would end. I didn't go back to Evella's house. I drove straight to my mother's house. My spirit had revealed the reason for my torment. My life was compiled of my truck, my TV and eight trash bags of clothes. I didn't have a pot to piss in, so to speak. I had never had a home of my own. I had never stood up and taken care of me. I had never created a life for myself. I had never stopped trying to ride someone else's coattails. I needed to make my own wind, to stand up and be a man. Not that I was sure what that meant exactly, but I knew change would take me forward.

When I got to my mother's house I was excited. I convinced her to let me come back and stay with her one last time. I told my mother, "This is it. I've got it figured out this time."

I stayed with my mother for about a year. It was a good year. I commuted fifty miles to work each way and never doubted the reason. The times I spent looking for my first apartment made it more than worthwhile. I had rented a room once, but this was a place I could call home. There was definitely some satisfaction in seeing my room at mom's place filled with pots, pans, sheets, towels, glasses, plates, a shower curtain and a bed. I also put a dresser on layaway. Every time I looked at that dresser I let out a sigh of relief. I had climbed a mountain and the view was brand new.

The shift was on, and I received my first promotion at what was turning out to be my best job ever. There I met Jann Horton. Jann would become a gift from God that stories could be written about. Only Christ can give the perfect gift and prepare your heart to receive it. He knew what I needed and when to give it to me, though the process had only just begun.

One day I was making my daily trip to the liquor store, and as I was getting out of the car—one foot on the ground and a foot on the brake, one hand on the wheel and a hand on the door—I remembered. I remembered that God remembered the Israelites were still wandering the desert. I wondered if He would remember me. It was worth a shot, so I offered my prayer: "God, I know I'm still Keith, and I know you're still God. I need some help with this alcohol thing. I can't do it on my own, but I think there could be hope. Whatever you have to do, whatever the consequences, I need your help so I can stop drinking." Afterwards I went in the store and got my bottle like I did every day. I never gave the prayer a second thought.

About two weeks later I was driving home from the beach at midnight on a Saturday. I had no reason to be out driving. I should have stayed where I was. But I had to let Jann's dogs out because she was out of town for the weekend. What I would learn later was that she awaited a breakthrough while contemplating my future in her life. At some point, as I was driving around the Beltway, the police decided they would help me out and give me a ride. The instant I saw the police lights in the rearview mirror something washed over me. I knew this was the time and this was the place. I was going to have to make a decision. I decided on sobriety, and it changed my life.

That prayer opened a door that I was ready to walk through. That's what I believe.

It was like I had awakened from a dream life. It completely opened up opportunities for me that I never thought were possible: things like a positive, healthy relationship; travel;

credit; and a new suit—you know, grown-up stuff.

I know there are people who don't believe in supernatural power and the hand of God. I tell you I understand now what it means to be born again. My life started anew and I was a new creature, a different human being. God was giving me another chance and I was ready. Love is the only foundation that matters when you're building on what God has given you. Jann and I were married about eighteen months later.

The first sign of my new beginning came about a month after the honeymoon. The truck my parents had helped me buy was dying. I had to have transportation in order to keep my job. This was our first decision as husband and wife. I was waiting for a mistake from my past to drop in and stop me before I could get started. What happened was my first glimpse at faith.

My truck was not worth fixing. To my surprise, Jann said, "You should get another truck." This was a great idea for about five minutes. Then I realized that buying a truck meant getting a loan. Things were turning around for me, but my past was always lurking.

What would Jann think when she found out my credit was bottom rung at best? This is where love comes in. She had me join her credit union and apply for a car loan all in the same day. The next day the credit union called and approved me for up to a $15,000 car loan. That red Jeep Cherokee is truly the truck Christ bought for me.

When you hear people say things like this, remember that it could be true.

Only Christ

My saltwater fish hobby allowed me to stay busy, focused and constructive. I would spend some of my free time sitting in the basement with the 200 total gallons of tanks and read books on faith, prophecy and the gospels. I had come a long way in my life, but something was telling me the best was yet to come. Something was coming my way; this I knew for sure. I have learned that just because you can't see something doesn't mean it isn't there. If you want to follow Christ and be connected to the spirit, then you walk by faith and not by sight.

On October 3, 2006 I received a phone call from Katrina, my youngest daughter's mother.

It seems Pearl had gotten into some trouble and her mother was bringing her to northern Virginia to stay with her sister. Pearl's mother wanted to let me know she would be enrolling Pearl in school on Friday of that same week. I told her to tell me the place and I would be there.

* * *

Pearl's mother called on Friday to say they needed a ride to Pearl's new school. I was at work at the time but this issue needed my attention, so I left work and went to Pearl's aunt's house to pick them up. I had some questions, but I wasn't sure they were worth asking. It was only a few months ago that I heard from Pearl for the first time in thirteen years. I really didn't know that much about my daughter, but I knew this could be a great opportunity.

By the time we got to the school, I had decided that a humble approach would serve me best. I told Pearl's mother that I would sit by the window and she could call me if she needed any help. That call never came but what I heard was interesting enough. The school administrator told Pearl's mother that Pearl could not stay with her aunt and go to school there. It seems Pearl's mother wanted to drop Pearl at her sister's house and go back to her home in another state.

This was a classic *What would Jesus do?* moment.

I asked Pearl's mother, "Why can't she stay with me and go to school? She is my daughter."

Pearl's mother was surprised at my suggestion. Her response was to question my authority to make such an offer. I called Jann to confirm my ability to back up my claim of help for those in need. Then I called on God. Once I called on my rock, my salvation, the pathway cleared for the reunion of father and child. I saw what was coming down the path of life, and was I ready. He must have thought so, because on October 8, 2006, Pearl became a member of our home. I only saw her once in thirteen years, but I knew this was the right thing to do.

That was a monumental day in several ways, and all of them made the day special. October 8 was Jann's and my sixth wedding anniversary. What would be the odds of two events of that magnitude happening to the same person on the same day? This is where you have to choose to believe, because it can't just be a coincidence. But because everything happens for a reason, I believe only Christ can do things like that. Wait—Wait—There's more from that day. Jann and I were in Manhattan that weekend celebrating our anniversary and we saw the Broadway play, *The Lion King*. While we were walking down Times Square, we saw the Ed Sullivan Theater.

I said to Jann, "Look, look, that's where they tape the *David Letterman Show*."

Jann said, "Let's go inside. There's a sign that says you can sign up for a chance to be in the audience."

So we went in the lobby, which looked like an old movie theater. There was a young lady there greeting people and encouraging them to sign up to have a chance to be picked to be in the audience for the taping. Jann and I signed the sheet and looked around the lobby for a while. We watched the show on TV at home, so it was pretty cool to be even this close.

We continued walking down Times Square admiring the city. "Look at this—look at that," I would say. I might as well have been six years old and at Disney World rather than a grown man seeing Times Square for the first time. (The next day we were leaving New York because we had to return home to pick up Pearl at her aunt's house.) But as we were driving home on October 8 they called and asked if we could be there that day for the taping of the show. We looked at each other in disbelief, but we had to say no. We had committed ourselves to pick up Pearl at a certain time and would not start this relationship by being late or postponing it.

Pearl had a very hard time adjusting to her new environment. She never saw this new set of circumstances as an opportunity. For her it was more of a burden. I believe Pearl wanted to change her past behavior and move on to a new way of life, but change was hard for her and she couldn't or wouldn't make the necessary effort to change her behavior. She became defiant in the face of any type of authority.

I, on the other hand, was excited at the opportunity

to make a difference for this child. I was out of her life for thirteen years, but with Christ at the helm there is always time. However, His time is not our time. We don't know how much time we have for any season in our life. That's why the faith we have in Christ carries us through every season. Whether it is a good season or bad, the thing you must remember is that when it is over you should not forget how or why you made it through. If you forget how you received the good and the bad, you won't understand the true meaning of *God with us*; for truly the kingdom of heaven is within us all. Christ is within us all if we choose to believe that He can and will do what His Word says.

Where the spirit goes the body must follow, and vice versa. Pearl's mind wanted to go where her eyes could see and not be concerned with the consequences. The world today has so many distractions, she could care less what I had to say.

This philosophy does not sit well with most parents, and there were many clashes of our conflicting views. There were no winners or losers, only contentious combatants who grew wearier after every encounter. It was a spiritual battle that went on for about two years between Pearl and Jann and me.

Jann and I were sure that the spirit of Christ would overtake any confusion that Pearl may have had about the nature of our conflict. However, Pearl's mind could only see that she must flee in order to be the person that she wanted to be. And in the middle of the night she did just that. She climbed out of her bedroom window and never looked back. My prayers these days are that she gains a renewed spirit. I can only hope that we lit a candle in Pearl and that that light will lead her to the spirit. The spirit will be waiting as if she never left. Because within is the kingdom of Heaven.

I've spent the past two years in therapy trying to grasp what happened that night Pearl left. Even though I know I did all I could do, I felt I should have been able to do more. I never looked at those events as though Christ couldn't do for Pearl what I had hoped. I know that one of two things happened: either I did something wrong, or Christ was holding the hands of the clock tied behind his back. Only He will say when it is time. We must continue on and be about His work.

Faith Personified

It's only recently that I really understood the therapeutic nature of having a hobby. I feel my saltwater fish hobby allows me to visualize an achievement or accomplishment that I have control over. I prepare and maintain the habitat for saltwater fish and coral. The feeling of accomplishment comes when the coral grows. They thrive and double in size. The same feeling of satisfaction comes when you have fish bred in captivity. It's the same with any other hobby that people have, as long as the hobby is constructive.

Periodically the water in the tanks must be changed. This is done so the chemical balance is maintained within the ecosystem. The saltwater tank is truly a living, breathing hobby. One day I was doing a little aqua-scaping and cleaning the tanks. I cleaned the glass top, wiped the 270-watt light bulb off, and then started moving the rocks around. And in a flash someone was calling my name.

"Keith, come with me."

"Keith!"

"Your time grows nigh and I have much to tell you."

"And bring the rock."

I couldn't tell if I was in a daze or this place was in a fog. I got to my feet and started down some kind of path. The place looked familiar, but if I'd been there before it wasn't during a time that I could remember.

"Where am I? This looks like a dream I've had," I said.

He tells me that I have great tasks ahead of me. So we need to keep moving. He also tells me, "This requires that you be able to watch, listen, hear and see as you move about the world. You have only to believe."

"Where are we going? Where're we headed?" I asked.

"We're taking a walk so I can explain a few things to you," He said.

"And, you are?" I finally asked. "Who are you and where are we?" I shouted.

"I am He who sent me," He said.

"What?" I asked.

He said, "There are few that have had the faith over the years, and been put through as much as you have. It is now time for you to use what you have been given. You've always known He has a plan for you and that time has come."

"The time for what has come?" I asked.

He told me, "The time draws near for *all* to be fulfilled and as you well know there is always work to be done."

"What does that have to do with me and who is He?" I asked.

"I am He," He told me.

The silence was only broken by my blank stare. I decided to go back to a previous question.

"Where are we? Is this a dream?" I asked.

"We are manifested in your spirit. We are in the Kingdom. You are cleaning your fish tank. That's why you can't drop the rock. We are in that place where you pray. That place where you are connected to the spirit of the Lord."

This is what He told me.

"I am the He who responds to your prayers. I am the one who Grace is bestowed upon to continually manifest your faith. When words are written about Christ and God—the Trinity in any part—He will be capitalized in response to Him. I am that He," He said.

"I reside in the kingdom and I'm manifested by your measured faith. You have been given an extreme measure for your purpose. That is the time that has come. When I said *all*, that meant you, too. Christ has grasped the book and the end grows nigh. During this time you will be charged with finding those who cannot find themselves. We will walk these last days together. You will be recognized as someone familiar to all who want to be saved but cannot find their way," He said.

"How will I find these people?" I asked.

"We will send them to you. They will find you. Their spirit will tell them you are familiar to them, but they will not know why. Once you speak Christ to them they will be made whole and saved for the day of days. There is one thing that will remain constant because the balance must be preserved. The Evil one has his measure as well, given to him by the Father. You can be recognized in the flesh, but their path must be discerned by the spirit. So, only when you speak Christ to them will they be able to find the path. You will have to discern if He has sent them, or the Enemy," He said.

"How many are there? How much time do we have? Are they all over the world or just in Virginia?" I asked.

"These things will be revealed to you as they always have, at the time they are needed. You have been given much, and much will be required. But, know that no measure that will be given unto you will be larger than the vessel that will carry it. Now drop the rock!" He said.

"Wait!" I screamed like a little girl.

"How will I get back, and what about Jann?" I said.

He said, "She's coming now, so I have to go. Remember, what is given to you by the Father is for you, so be wary of the helper who knows the answer. Now go and let the light lead the way."

"Keith! What are you doing? Why can't you answer me?" Jann was yelling as she was coming down the steps into the basement.

"What happened? Are you ok?" she asked.

"I'm not sure, give me a minute." I said. "What's up and why are you yelling?"

"You're taking your head out of the fish tank and you're asking me questions. We'll get back to that, but someone is here to see you," Jann said.

"Good point," I said.

I took a look around to make sure where I was, then grabbed a towel and told Jann that I'd be right there. I dried off my arms and face and headed upstairs to see who had come to see me without calling first. That doesn't happen very often, so something was definitely up. I knew it wasn't the police or Jann would have said that that's who it was. The first thing I looked for when I got to the top of the stairs was the car out front. I saw a limousine in the driveway. Now there's something you don't see every day. Before I could make an assumption about who was in my kitchen, John was introducing himself.

"Hello, my name is John Steadfast. Are you Keith W. Rustin Jr.?" He asked.

"Yes," I answered.

He reached into a folder and handed me some papers and asked, "Did you write that autobiographical summary?"

"Yes," I said.

It had my name on it and my favorite saying as the title: "Lessons repeat themselves until learned." It was definitely mine.

John said, "I represent the Eternal Flame Publishing Company. I was sent to offer you the opportunity to share your story with all the people who need to be told the story of redemption."

"Where did you get my story?" I asked.

"If you accept the offer, you can ask my boss. He is the one who sent me," John said.

Now that sounds familiar.

I told myself, "You're darn right that sounds familiar. I just had a near-death experience or a vision from Christ. I'm not sure which, but this can't be a coincidence. But that guy said He sent Him, too. I've written some of my life's lessons and failures, but only Christ knows my whole story. So, if John has my story, does that mean he got it from Christ? That would or could mean He is a manifestation of Christ."

Wow!

This would take a great deal of faith to comprehend, and yet, comprehension is not a prerequisite for faith. You only need to believe.

It would take some time to sort out the day's events, but I was not about to pass up a chance to share my story with people who wanted to be redeemed as I was.

"Mr. Steadfast," I said, "I would love to hear what your

boss has to say. Can I ask a question?"

"Of course," John said.

"What is your boss's name?" I asked.

John said, "His name is Mr. Yahweh. Mr. Yahweh is the publisher of the Eternal Flame Publishing Company."

"Do you mean Mr. Yahweh, the counselor?" I asked.

"Mr. Yahweh is many things to many people," John told me. "He will teach you all you need to know about the journey ahead."

"What happens next, now that Faith has been made whole? Christ has answered my prayer far beyond anything I could have imagined by you showing up."

John said this to me: "During this time, you will be charged with finding those who cannot find themselves. As you have been told before, your faith is worthy of the task."

It confirmed what my spirit already knew.

www.ingramcontent.com/pod-product-compliance
Lightning Source LLC
LaVergne TN
LVHW020940090426
835512LV00020B/3437